Unleash Your

AIRBNB REVENUE

*How To Make The Most Money
On Your First Airbnb listing*

By

David Leroux

Table Of Contents

Chapter 1: Introduction 4

Chapter 2: How Do I Get Started? 6

Chapter 3: How To Create a Successful Airbnb listing
that stands out 10

Chapter 4: Essentials for Your Home 20

Chapter 5: Welcoming Your First Guest 28

Chapter 6: Keeping Records And Sticking To Airbnb Rules 32

Chapter 7: Getting Sterling Reviews, And Handling Bad Ones 34

Chapter 8: How to Price Your Listing to Earn So Much More 39

Chapter 9: Getting Paid 44

Conclusion 47

Are you interested in buying the top 1% of the most profitable Airbnb investment properties while complying to Airbnb cities regulations?

Register to my FREE online workshop at www.cashflowstreet.com

Chapter 1
Introduction

What is Airbnb?

If you're reading this you probably already have a vague idea of what Airbnb is. Airbnb and other similar room-rental schemes such as Homeaway, and Booking.com are some of the best and most innovative uses of the Internet and help you make money from your biggest asset, your home.

Born out of older sites such as couch-surfer and the old student and hippy tradition of crashing on the sofa wherever you can find one; Airbnb takes it to another level. It allows you to rent out your spare rooms or indeed properties to travelers allowing them to stay somewhere friendly, homely and usually cheaper than if they were to stay in a hotel.

While it started off as a way for friends to find somewhere to stay in San Francisco, it has now spread around the world with millions of people opening their homes to strangers, making new friends and making a bit of extra money as a bonus.

The author and his wife have made over tens of thousands in the last three years with over 100 5-star rated reviews on our average suburban home and I want to give you the best chance to do the same. If you frequently travel around, you know very well that accommodation is not cheap. Checking into a hotel can cost you a few hundred dollars per night.

With this being said, you should realize that the lodging industry is lucrative and can help you make extra money. You can rent out your home or spare rooms to vacationers and tourists via Airbnb.

Airbnb is a popular lodging option for tourists and travelers. It was originally called Airbed & Breakfast and founded by Joe Gebbia and Brian Chesky in 2008.

The official website of Airbnb serves as a virtual community that connects hosts and travelers with one another.

When you sign up and become a member, you can put your home in a listing and rent it out for a short period of time. The payment is sent to Airbnb, which takes a small cut from it.

Thanks for downloading this book. It's my firm belief that it will provide you with all the answers to your questions.

Chapter 2
How Do I Get Started?

The first question you need to ask yourself before diving into Airbnb hosting is this: "Do I have the right personality to be an Airbnb host?"

In my opinion, personality plays a critical role in determining how much you will enjoy being an Airbnb host and how profitable your little enterprise will become.

If you have the type of personality that people tend to call "bubbly," "engaging," "outgoing," "extroverted" or "friendly," you probably have what it takes to be a genuinely warm and welcoming host.

You may be a natural at hosting if:

1) You tend to trust rather than fear.
2) You tend to give strangers the benefit of the doubt.
3) You enjoy engaging in conversation with people you've never met.
4) You enjoy helping others.
5) You enjoy hosting family and friends when they visit from out of town.
6) You're flexible and adapt easily to change.
7) You don't mind sharing.
8) You're open minded and curious about the world.
9) You enjoy meeting people from different cultures.

Let's start by addressing the first two traits in this list.

Many people ask me how to become an Airbnb host, but I can tell from their line of questioning whether or not they will actually follow through. Some ask me downright bizarre questions, such as, "How do you know your guest won't load all your possessions into a truck and take off?" or "How do you know your guest isn't an axe murderer who will hack you to death in your bed?"

Wow. Okay.

When I hear shocking questions like this, I can tell that fear of strangers will probably prevent them from ever being Airbnb hosts. They are too afraid to share their space. They also may be too afraid to let a traveler stay at their home even if they are out of town during the visit. Their fear is so overpowering they can't imagine opening their door and allowing a traveler to enter.

Let's talk about "stranger danger." Just about every day we hear media stories about strangers kidnapping children and teens. Reality-based stories about serial killers, con artists, thieves and swindlers are constant fodder for television shows and movies. People all over the world have become conditioned to fear people they don't know.

Airbnb, on the other hand, is based on trust and a sense of community. The very essence of Airbnb flies in the face of stranger danger. The great thing about Airbnb is that it enables strangers to meet and get to know each other virtually before they ever meet in real life. Guests can read reviews other travelers have written about the host. Hosts can read reviews other Airbnb hosts have written about guests.

As a host, you will be able to read messages from your potential guests, view their photos, read their online profiles, read reviews written about them by other hosts, and see how many different ways Airbnb has verified their identities. If these methods are not sufficient to help you overcome your fear of strangers, then Airbnb hosting may not be the right choice for you.

Similarly, if you are so introverted that you tend to avoid eye contact with others and find it painfully awkward to engage in small talk, then you probably don't have the right personality to make guests feel welcome in your home. I'm not saying that introverts can't be Airbnb hosts. I love introverts. Sometimes they're so shy it's adorable, and they tend to be thoughtful, perceptive, unique individuals with deep thoughts. I'm simply pointing out that if you tend to be shy and fearful of social interactions, you may need to make an extra effort to come out of your shell. Greet your guests with a firm handshake and a big smile. Practice small talk. Start with these two lines: "Welcome! How was your trip?"

Imagine how you'd feel as a traveler entering someone's home for the first time. You'd want to be reassured that you're welcome there, right? You'd want the host to look you in the eye, smile, and greet you with enthusiasm. You'd want the guest's whole demeanor and body language to say, "Welcome to my home. Come on in. Make yourself comfortable. Relax. Your long journey is finally over. A hot shower and wonderful bed await you."

Flexibility is another important personality trait. You need to be flexible enough to deal with the unexpected. Sometimes guests need to cancel because their plans change. Sometimes a new guest will ask for a last-minute booking and arrive a few hours later. Sometimes a guest will want to leave a day early or check out a day later. My advice is: go with the flow. We can't predict the future. We can only be here now, in the present moment. Relax and bend. Remember that those who aren't flexible are likely to get bent out of shape.

Being open-minded is also important. As a host, you need to be comfortable interacting with people from all over the world and from different cultural backgrounds. Knowing other languages is a plus, but it's not necessary. Just speak slowly and clearly and use a lot of hand gestures to get your point across. Keep in mind that a smile is a universal way to make guests feel welcome. Some cultures value silence and privacy. Others value connection and conversation. Pay attention to social cues from your guests and try to adapt to their rhythms.

If you feel you have the right personality to enjoy hosting, let's move on and talk about the nitty-gritty of what it takes to get started.

Getting Started in Seven Steps

It's easy to get started as a host on Airbnb, but it does require some time and energy. You'll need both mental and physical energy to tackle these seven steps:

1) De-clutter and clean your space.
2) Take clear, well-lit photos.
3) Write a great description of your space.
4) List the amenities you offer.
5) Describe your neighborhood.
6) Write excellent directions.
7) Create a profile and add your photo.

Chapter 3
How To Create a Successful Airbnb listing that stands out

Registering with Airbnb

First, you will need to register with Airbnb using an active Facebook account, Google account or a valid email.

On the next page, you will need to enter your first name, last name, email address and a password. Next, enter your real birthday. This is a part of what makes Airbnb a safe marketplace. Next, click the "sign up" button. On the next page, you will have the option to indicate how you first learned about Airbnb.

After providing all this information, you will receive an email asking you to confirm your email address. Once you do that, you will be redirected to your profile page. This is a great time to add a profile photo and complete your profile. By clicking on the "add profile photo," you can either upload a photo from your computer or take a picture with your webcam. A great photo is an important aspect of building comfort and confidence with prospective guests.

Next, you need to fill out your profile information. The more information you provide, the better your bookings will be. Trust starts with transparency. You will be asking your guests for deposits, so you want to make sure that you are providing them with enough information about you for them to feel comfortable about booking your space and sending you money.

The next section of your profile is called "Trust and Verification." Click on "Verify Me" and provide the information from your official government ID.

Verify your phone number by entering your phone number and choosing to be verified by either a text message or an automated phone call.

Now you are ready to set up your accommodation listings.

Completing Your Accommodation Listing

The great news is that you don't have to complete your listing in one setting. If you can't come up with a headline or do not like the description that you create you can save the profile without publishing it and come back to it later. You can also change or update the description of your listing as you introduce new amenities or change some features.

As with any other business, when listing your property on Airbnb, you want to make sure that you have a price that is reasonable and competitive for your specific location.

This is why before creating your listing you might want to take a look at accommodations in your area listed by other hosts.

Go to Airbnb homepage, enter the name of your city, choose dates, select the number of guests that your property will comfortably accommodate and hit "Search."

In the search results narrow the type of accommodations. If you are offering a room, see at what rates other rooms are available. Airbnb has an interactive map that you can use to review properties in the vicinity of your space.

Review the listing and note the amenities and services offered by your future competition. You want to pay special attention to the size of the beds and size of TVs. Also, check what's offered in the kitchen if there is one and what is the parking situation.

While there is no size fits all kind of promotion you can do on Airbnb, if all your competitors offer free parking, and you don't, you will definitely need to compensate for it with some additional features or amenities of your apartment.

To get started with listing a property, click on the "Become a Host" button. From here select the home type, the room type and then how many people the accommodation will hold. Then type in your city.

On the next page add the number of bedrooms, the number of bed and the number of bathrooms.

Indicate the property type and the room type.

Creating a Listing Name

Now it's time to enter your Listing Headline or Listing Name. A Listing Name can be up to 35 characters long. The headline will appear in your guests' search results and many different places in your Airbnb host portal.

Your listing headline is your chance to make a great first impression, so make sure you come up with a creative message that stands out from the competition.

Here are some really bad examples of listing headlines:

Comfy Apartment – doesn't really describe anything specific about your accommodation

Great Glen Cove Apartment – this is what all Glen Cove hosts are going to say about their apartments

In the same category are:

The Best Airbnb Rental

Country Living

Remote Cabin

Here are a few examples of really great, unique, catchy headlines:

Runners Dream in Boulder

Central Astoria Family Townhome

Dogs love this backyard!

When creating a headline, use words that describe key benefits of your accommodation. Here are some pointers for you:

Property type – room, apartment, condo, house

Proximity to a hot tourist spot – downtown, next to the Metropolitan Museum of Art, etc.

Hints about your policies, especially if your property is child or pet-friendly

You can also offer information about specific amenities, such as a hot tub, basketball court, gym or swimming pool

Do not mention the following in your headline:

- Name of the city
- Number of bedrooms
- Number of guests allowed

All these things are covered elsewhere in your profile, and you don't want your listing headline to talk about things that are mentioned elsewhere.

Property Summary

The next most important part of your listing after the headline is the property summary. It can be up to 250 characters long. Most likely your prospective guests are looking at several properties at the same time. Their attention span is very short, and it is possible that they will not read the entire description right away. This is why you want to have great and catchy property summary. You also want to present the information in your profile in bite size, not as a story or a novel.

Here is a template that you can use:

The Glen Cove Townhome is a well-equipped and spacious 2 bedroom location with an incredible location. Enjoy luxury bedding, a Jacuzzi, 70' flat screen TV, and a full kitchen. Experience Long Island with at-home comfort, security, and privacy.

Description Page

The description page in your listing profile will also have a line that says "You can add more details to tell travelers about your space and hosting style."

Clicking on the word "details" will open a new section of the page that allows you to add details about your space and hospitality.

Here's what you can write about here:

The space

Guest Access

Interaction with Guests

House Rules

The Neighborhood – Overview

The Neighborhood – Getting Around

Address

You will then need to type the address of your accommodation. Make sure that the pin on the map is in the correct location.

Amenities page

Next, use the amenities checkboxes to show guest what your apartment has to offer. Here are the amenities that Airbnb is going to ask you about:

Essentials

TV

Cable TV

Air Conditioning

Heating

Kitchen

Internet

Wireless Internet

Hot Tub

Washer

Pool

Dryer

Breakfast

Free Parking on Premises

Gym

Elevator in Building

Indoor Fireplace

Buzzer/Wireless Intercom

Doorman

Shampoo

Special features:

Family/kid friendly

Smoking allowed

Suitable for events

Pets allowed

Pets live on this property

Wheelchair accessible

Pricing

As discussed elsewhere, you need to start with researching your competition to see what the prices of comparable accommodations are.

You also need to remember that not the entire amount that your guests pay for your listing will end up in your pocket. You will have added expenses such as housekeeping, amenities, Airbnb fee. In addition to this, there will be a percentage of the time when your rental will simply sit vacant.

Before you set your rates, consider the following:

-   Will it be a supplementary income or a primary income for you?

-   Who will be doing the housekeeping? Can you commit to doing it yourself? If not and you need to hire someone, how much will it cost?

-   Assess the total cost of preparing the space for each new guest, including the amenities, laundry costs and cleaning supplies. Also don't forget to think about the cost of electricity, water, gas, heat and subscription services such as Netflix.

Here is a formula that you can use to get started with your Airbnb rental price:

Take the monthly market rent of your apartment.

Divide it by 30. You will get typical daily rent.

Double this number and use it as your Airbnb starting rate.

Prices, competition and the number of bookings may significantly change depending on a season of the year or even something as unpredictable as bad news coming from your area.

Photos of your property

Photos of your property are the most important part of your listing. You can create great compelling copies because it will be the photos that will make someone really want to stay at your property.

Airbnb offers free professional photography in select metropolitan areas. If it's available, apply right away. Ask them to shoot your property at the highest resolution possible. In the meantime, you can upload your own pictures and replace them with the professional ones when they are ready.

When taking pictures yourself, never shoot them in portrait mode. Always shoot them in landscape. Before taking the pictures clean the property thoroughly. Stage the rooms by removing clutter. Add small touches such as flowers. Open blinds and curtains to allow natural light to illuminate the space. Don't forget to take pictures of special features such as a patio or Jacuzzi tub.

After you take the pictures, show them to your friends and family and ask for feedback.

Before you upload the photos, put some thinking into the sequence. Think about how you want your guests to experience your accommodation.

Airbnb supports unlimited photos at no additional cost. Here are a few technical requirements:

- Use JPEG/JPG format

- Photos should be under 7MB in size per photo

Home Safety Card

Next section in your Airbnb listing profile is Home Safety Card.

This is a handy resource to keep in your listing, because it tells guests about the location of a fire extinguisher, fire alarm and gas shutoff valve. It also gives emergency exit instructions and provides emergency phone numbers.

The final step is indicating when your accommodation space is available. If you are going to make it available anytime, then simply select "Always." If you plan on making your property available from time to time, then choose "Sometimes." If you are only making your place available once, select "One-time" option.

The listing is now ready to go live.

Chapter 4
Essentials for Your Home

Every home is different – be it the size, location or character. Nonetheless, there are essential items that every home listed on Airbnb should possess.

Below is a list of items to consider stocking in your Airbnb. Some places simply won't need certain items (e.g. heaters in Hawaii) but the following represents a comprehensive list that should prevent your guests from ever saying "I wish this place had a dot-dot-dot".

For each item, you should strive to find something that satisfies the following home furnishing purchasing principles:

- Price: Given the sea of consumer options these days, why pay more for something you can get for less?
- Functionality: Does the item do what your guests would want, need and expect it to do?
- Quality: Spend the extra couple of bucks on buying items that elevate your home furnishings, amenities and hospitality standards.
- Durability: You're in the short-term home rental game. Make sure your purchases will withstand the test of time.
- Replaceability: Accidents inevitably happen. How easy/hard would it be to replace that one smashed plate?
- Neutrality: Your guests come in all shapes, colors and sizes. Pick unobjectionable items, colors and styles that are agreeable to most.

For the Entire Home

- Air freshener, potpourri or scented reed diffusers
- Air mattress
- Baby crib

- Broom and dustpan
- Doormat
- First aid kit
- High-speed Wi-Fi internet
- Magic eraser
- Mop and bucket
- Multi-purpose surface spray
- Phone charging cables
- Scrub sponges
- Toolkit
- Universal travel electrical adapters
- Vacuum cleaner
- Whiteboard

Bedrooms

- Alarm clock
- Bed
- Bed linen
- Bedside table
- Blackout curtains, shades or blinds

- Chest of drawers / dresser
- Duvet / comforter
- Duvet cover
- Extra blankets
- Ear plugs and eye masks
- Full-length mirror
- Good pillows
- Hangers
- Mattress
- Mattress protector
- Portable fan and heater
- Reading lamp
- Tissues (and tissue box cover)
- Throw pillows
- Wall clock

Bathrooms

- Bath mat
- Bath towels
- Body wash / shower gel
- Disposable razors
- Earbuds (Q-Tips)

- Full length mirror
- Hair dryer
- Hand soap
- Hand towels
- Hooks and towel racks
- Shampoo and conditioner
- Shaving cream
- Tissues
- Toilet brush
- Toilet paper
- Toilet plunger
- Toothbrush and toothpaste holder
- Toothpaste
- Trash Can

Dining Room

- Coasters
- Dining room chairs
- Dining room table
- Napkins
- Napkin holder

- Placemats

Laundry

- Clothes drying rack
- Dryer
- Iron
- Ironing board
- Laundry detergent and softener
- Laundry hamper
- Washing machine

Living Room

- Coasters
- Coffee table
- Lounge room chairs
- Media players
- Sofa
- Smart TV
- Streaming media services (e.g. Amazon Prime Instant Video, Hulu Plus, iTunes, Netflix)

Kitchen

- Aluminum foil
- Anti-bacterial surface
- Cleaner spray
- Baking paper
- Can opener
- Coffee maker and coffee supplies
- Cutting boards
- Dinnerware set
- Dishwashing soap
- Disinfectant wipes
- Garbage bags
- Glassware set
- Hand soap
- Kettle
- Knife set
- Ladles
- Microwave

- Olive oil
- Paper towels
- Plastic cling wrap
- Pots and pans set
- Salt and pepper
- Serving spoons
- Silverware (cutlery) set
- Spice rack (and spices)
- Sugar
- Trash can
- Toaster
- Tongs
- Tupperware set

Are you interested in buying the top 1% of the most profitable Airbnb investment properties while complying to Airbnb cities regulations?

Register to my FREE online workshop at www.cashflowstreet.com

Chapter 5
Welcoming Your First Guest

If you are going to share the space with your guests, it helps to be there to open the door when they arrive and personally welcome them into your home. If you have the time, pick them up at the airport, train station or nearest transit stop. I often walk from my place to the nearest transit stop so I can greet my guests when they disembark and personally accompany them to my place. If it's raining, I bring an umbrella large enough to cover both of us.

When guests walk into your home, show them to their room right away. Turn on the light in the bathroom so they can see it clearly. Both the bedroom and bathroom should be clean, with fresh towels on the towel bar and fresh sheets on the beds. The two things that guests are most eager to receive when they arrive are the key and instructions on how to access the Internet, so be sure to give them those things first.

Next, show them the basics, such as which shelf of the refrigerator they can use, how to make coffee and tea, and how to use the TV remote. It's also nice to be there in person so you can ask them if they have any questions. When they have run out of questions, it's good to conclude by asking, "Is there anything else I can do for you right now?"

Often guests are tired, preoccupied and not in a social mood when they arrive. They may have plans to drop their bags, take a quick shower, and go out to eat. I can usually tell if guests are in a hurry to get to their next destination. At these times, I simply hand them their keys, go over a few basics, let them know they can text me if they have any questions, and quickly get out of their way.

If you can't be home and the guest will enter your property using the key in your lockbox, you can still be present in spirit by providing a welcome letter and instructions that let them know everything they need to know to access the Internet and find their way around your kitchen and living room. Post little welcome notes with your guests' names on them so they'll still feel welcomed by you, even if you're at work or elsewhere.

I always tape notes to the guest room doors so they know where to go. I do this every time, no matter what. For example, I'll write, "Hilda's Room" or "Bathroom for Geraldine and Dagwood" or "Welcome, Izzy and Whizzy." Seeing their names on the door make my guests feel as if they belong there, as if they own that room and the room was waiting eagerly for them to enter it.

If your guests arrived during your absence, be sure to call out, "Hello! Is anyone here?" when you get home.

I do this because it usually prompts guests to come out of their rooms into the shared living spaces so I can shake their hands and personally welcome them to my home.

Orienting your guests

Help your guest figure out where they are and how to settle into your place by leaving maps, guidebooks, and brochures about nearby tourist attractions on their nightstand or other table in their bedroom. Some people refer to the information sheet as the "house rules," but that term sounds rather stern and parental to me. I prefer to label my two information sheets, "Dear Upstairs Guest" and "Dear Downstairs Guest."

I also place notes in strategic places. For example, I label my recycling bins and trash can so guests know where to discard plastic, paper, glass and refuse. Beside the kitchen faucet, I have posted a laminated sign explaining that they don't need to worry about washing their dishes: they can simply rinse them and load them in the dishwasher, which I periodically run.

The next step is to help them get oriented by reviewing the neighborhood map you've created for them. Often travelers arrive in the dark and have no idea exactly where they are. They usually have a vague idea from having seen a small star on a small online map indicating your location, but that's about it.

I create my neighborhood map by going to Google maps and zooming in to the point at which the local street names are visible. I print out the map in color and then add information with a black felt pen. I periodically make more copies, as needed, for new guests. Most guests take the maps with them, so I always print additional copies. I keep them in a folder labeled "Airbnb," along with my letters to my upstairs guests and downstairs guests.

There are many things you can do to make your guests feel welcome. Some hosts place chocolates or mints on the pillows. Because I'm not sure everyone likes chocolate, I place sealed squares of Ghiradelli chocolates in a small basket on the kitchen island with a handwritten note attached that says, "For My Airbnb Guests." If I bake brownies or lemon bars, I stack them on a plate, cover it with clear wrap, and set out a note that says, "Help Yourself! Baked by your Airbnb Host."

Make a Good First Impression

You want guests to walk into your space, look around in delight, smile and say, "Wow!"

Think of all those home remodeling shows on HGTV. What happens when the designer pulls off the blindfolds and the homeowners see their remodeled space for the very first time? Their eyes grow wide. Their mouths drop open. They cry out in astonishment. They gasp. They laugh. They shed tears of joy.

That is the level of happy excitement you should strive to evoke. I know, you're thinking to yourself, "There is no way that's going to happen when people walk into my house!" That may be true, but it's still a motivating goal to have in mind as you clean, organize, and decorate your space.

One of the best intangible benefits of being an Airbnb host is having a reason to keep your home clean and organized. Even when I have no guests staying with me, I feel good walking into my clutter-free, dust-free home. I can relax and thoroughly enjoy my space because I've prepared it so well to be an attractive, nurturing, comforting place to relax and hang out.

Chapter 6
Keeping Records And Sticking To Airbnb Rules

If you are even moderately successful with Airbnb, then it is well worth keeping certain basic records of who you have staying with you. Over the years, Airbnb (though not rival sites) have reduced the information that they provide with hosts ostensibly for our own security but in reality, it seems to be simply a pointless way to try and keep people from conducting transactions off the system. It can be annoying though as it can restrict you from easily obtaining pretty essential information that you might want if you ever have to file your taxes.

It's a good idea to get in the habit of keeping a log book whether on paper or on your computer using Excel or Numbers to record the names, contact addresses, telephone numbers of your guests and also the dates they stayed for, prices you charged and the income you received minus the Airbnb fees. Though Airbnb now hides some of this information, once a booking has been made then you can still request it from your guest before they arrive or while they are staying with you.

If there is one thing that Airbnb and other operators are tight on, it is swapping contact information and making bookings off the system. Understandably this is because, for every night booked through the Airbnb system, they take a small fee from the host and a larger fee from the guest. As a result, if you try and swap contact details before making a booking, Airbnb software algorithms will likely detect it and black out the information or block it entirely. Repeated attempts to beat the system may end up with either guest or host removed from the system.

If you do get someone trying to book outside the system, it's always wise to politely inform them you only make bookings through Airbnb. This way their ID is verified and you are covered by the insurance. Sometimes on very rare occasions, potential guests may want to view your property. To be honest, I always decline such guests but if you feel you want to do this, contact Airbnb and they can arrange a visit.

Of course being a great guest will likely mean that you make several friends and you'll have people wanting to stay with you again and again. Once you get to know your guest and they have stayed with you once or twice or perhaps, they book with you for a week and want to stay with you for longer or return another time then it is entirely up to you whether to make arrangements privately. It will save both parties money and can often be just easier for guest or host alike. Of course, you'd lose the Airbnb insurance and protection for subsequent visits but hopefully, you know your guests well enough to work out if this is going to be a problem and if it is…. there is always the Police! If you do take some bookings privately, do remember to keep your financial records up to date and block out your calendar on Airbnb to save you getting bombarded with inquiries that you can't accept.

Chapter 7
Getting Sterling Reviews, And Handling Bad Ones

At this point, we already know that the lifeblood of an Airbnb comes from great reviews. To be able to maintain sterling reviews, it's important for a host to understand how they're being reviewed.

A. How hosts are reviewed

Airbnb basically gives every guest 6 criteria: accuracy, communication, cleanliness, location, check-in and value. We'll go through the components of each and how to increase the likelihood of getting 5-star reviews for each category.

1. Accuracy of Listing

This is basically how close the reality your listing is. We painted a picture of your property through photos and a description – it should not be too far from the guest's actual experience.

To ensure accuracy in your listing:

   a. Call out some quirks and avoid surprises. There is no perfect Airbnb. Every listing has less-than-desirable features. Make a list of characteristics that you think may be off-putting to some guests. Neighbor's got a dog that barks at wee hours? Mattress tends to be a bit firm?
   b. Call this out in your profile. If the guest is aware before they arrive, then it shouldn't be a problem.
   c. Post great-looking but realistic pictures. Most guests tend to post all areas of the home, but you can choose to post just those that the guest has access to. The trick is to make the place recognizable, and not make the guest wonder as if it's a different house they ended up in.

d. Be thorough in your listing. Your Airbnb listing is there to give prospective guests a good idea of what it might be like to stay in your place. Guests look for different things during their stay, so being thorough counts.

2. Cleanliness and Hygiene

Some guests are easier to please than others, but a non-negotiable for all guests is the cleanliness of the place. Most guests travel long distances and just want a comfortable place to crash after their journey, so the last thing they want to walk into is a messy place.

   a. Provide guests with a welcoming home. Similar to when you stay at a hotel, you expect everything to be spic and span, and ready for use. Have the same standard for your listing.
   b. Give yourself enough time. It's fine to book back-to-back stays, but give yourself enough time between check-outs to do housekeeping. As we tackled in Section VII, it's best to do a time and motion so you have an idea how much time you'll need.

3. Communication

Airbnb will also ask the guest how responsive and accessible you were before and during the stay. To get your guest's favor on this category:

   a. Give them different ways to contact you. Airbnb's messenger is linked to your email, so if it's synced to your phone, then you should be able to answer inquiries readily. Once you get to communicating with a paid guest, give them another option such as voice calls. More often, a call will

address concerns more quickly than a back-and-forth of emails.
   b. Check-on your guest periodically. It's likely that everything is fine if your guest does not contact you, but being proactive will help you go above and beyond their expectations. Guests may sometimes feel that their concern is too minor to raise, so checking in will help you improve their stay.

4. Location

Airbnb will also ask your guests about the appeal of your neighborhood, in terms of safety, convenience and overall desirability. While this may seem beyond your control, there are ways to help your guests make the most of their stay in your neighborhood:

   a. Create an Airbnb Guidebook. As we discussed in Section III, the guidebook is one feature that is sure to impress guests. Remember that guests book Airbnb in order to get a feel of the neighborhood and be able to experience it like a local - having an easier time navigating your neighborhood will help your guest look upon it more favorably.
   b. Recommend transport options. Apart from the check-in, another factor that builds a guest's first impression of your listing is how easy it is to get to. Providing them with clear instructions on how to get to your place makes the neighborhood feel more accessible.

5. Value

Airbnb will ask guests if they feel that your listing was value for money.

   a. Add local flair and a few little touches. Remember our discussion in Section? We aimed to give the place a local flavor as well as some extras to make them feel more welcome. These little perks go a long way in impressing guests.

b. Offer discounts in the future. Whether your guests take it up or not, offering a discount or free night gives the current stay an increased perception of value. It may also get you additional bookings in the future.

6. Check-in Process

Apart from the listing, guests can also rate you on ease of check-in.

- A. Help guests get to your place. Your place may be glorious, but if your guest had a hard time getting to it, then that will most likely affect their first impression on you and the listing. Find out how your guest will be arriving and suggest the easiest way to get from the point of arrival to your place. Some hosts even provide step-by-step instructions with photos, just to be able to guide the guest.
- B. Escort the guest, and have someone meet them in person. It may not be possible all the time, but do consider hiring a concierge to welcome guests. Nothing beats having someone they trust be physically present when they arrive, and be able to assist them with their needs.
- C. Create a House Manual. As we tackled in Section VII, a house manual will help your guest navigate the house more easily, and when you're not around.

As you receive reviews, you'll also find that most guests leave constructive comments. Take each comment as a chance for you to improve your property and service.

B. How to handle bad reviews

At some point, there will either be a bad apple among your guests, or an unavoidable circumstance that may cause you to get a bad review. Whether you've encountered a guest who's impossible to please, or your service really did slip this time, it's not the end of your Airbnb business yet.

Have you ever noticed that there are hardly any bad reviews in Airbnb? Going back to the Airbnb algorithm, it's because hosts with bad reviews are pushed to the bottom end of the search list. Moreover, most hosts understand that reviews make or break a business, so they abide by the standards set by the company.

So if you do get a bad review, look at the bright side: mostly good reviews can arouse suspicion amongst prospective guests, and a bad review can balance this through a varied perspective. It can then lend some credibility to the good reviews.

Most importantly, it gives you a chance to respond. To show future guests that you care about their experience and feedback, the way to handle a bad review is through a sterling, well-crafted response. When you get a bad review, do the following:

1. Do not reply immediately. Take the time to breath and calm down.
2. Do not use a confrontational tone. Be as polite as possible, and acknowledge that you understand their feelings or concerns.
3. Do address each and every concern that the guest raised. If you can fix it, state how you plan to do so. If you feel that it was a misunderstanding or was improperly stated, provide your perspective.
4. Offer a subsequent stay with the issue fixed, at a discounted rate.

One or two bad reviews will not tarnish your reputation. It's all a matter of handling it with composure, and focusing on the coming guests who will appreciate your brand of service.

Chapter 8
How to Price Your Listing to Earn So Much More

Apart from taxes and legalities, pricing the property correctly is often an overwhelming and confusing part of the Airbnb business. But you shouldn't let the confusion and initial overwhelm deter you from mastering this part – this is actually where you make money.

Airbnb has a built-in pricing calculator, and there are also third-party pricing calculators out there. However, understanding some pricing principles will enable you to understand your business, and crunch numbers to make the most profit possible.

Simple math would tell us that to earn our $5,000 goal, you would have to make $162 per night and have all 31 nights booked.

AVERAGE NIGHTLY PRICE	# OF NIGHTS BOOKED	EARNINGS PER MONTH
$162	31	$5,000

Below, I will teach you how to: (1) determine if your property can be priced at this nightly rate, (2) ensure that your property is booked solid, (3) ways for you to price it higher.

Nightly Price

Once you list your property, you will be asked to give your asking price per night. The price you set is supposed to reflect the size, amenities, and location of your listing.

Airbnb's calculator will suggest a pricing tip based on listings similar to yours, and while you may start with that, I'd suggest making your own pricing down the line. The basis of Airbnb is very limited – what we're after here is your pad's profitability.

Airbnb's calculator will look at your location, size (number of bedrooms and baths), property type (apartment, condo, house), and number of guests you can accommodate.

The problem is that there are properties similar to yours in these aspects, but may not be the same quality as your property. You risk over or underpricing then.

Here's how to determine your nightly price:

Step 1: Look at the average nightly price of properties like yours.

Search on Airbnb for properties within your neighborhood, and be as specific as possible. For example, instead of typing Manhattan, New York, put Marble Hill, Manhattan. Then enter any date, and assume you're having an overnight stay.

Then, the Filter Options will show. Proceed to select all the filters that apply to your listing: room type, size, amenities and property type.

Your search will show you the number of listings in your neighborhood that are just like yours, and the average price nightly.

Step 2: Next, look at the average nightly price of properties like yours, for every month of the year.

The season and the number of listings available in your neighborhood should be part of the strategy for determining your pricing. Basically, when there is more demand (less properties available), price higher; when there is more supply (more properties available), price lower.

Fill up a chart with the following details:

MONTH	# OF LISTINGS	AVERAGE PRICE/NIGHT	YOUR PRICE

I suggest adjusting your price by deducting or adding 5-10% depending on the number of listings and average price per night in your neighborhood.

At the beginning, however, I would suggest that you price lower than your competition, just to get the bookings coming in first. Switch to the method above once you have several 5 star reviews.

Tip: Here's a step-by-step guide to Setting Your Base Price.

Special Offer

A Special Offer or simply a discount is a good way to keep your property occupied for longer. Now, you might be asking – wouldn't a discount hurt my earnings? Not if it means that you will have more nights booked.

Let's assume that once you offer a discount, you'll hook a one-week long stay:

WITH DISCOUNT		WITHOUT DISCOUNT	
Nightly Price	$162	Nightly Price	$162
Discount	0.10	Discount	-
Nightly stays / mo	17 or $2754	Nightly stays / mo	17 or $2754
Weekly stays / mo	2 or $2268	Weekly stays / mo	1 or $1134
NET INCOME	$5,022	NET INCOME	$3,888.00
	-502.20		
	$4,519.8		

Note that Airbnb counts a weekly stay if its lasts for at least 7 nights. The table above shows that even if you discount, if you keep your property booked, you'll still earn more than if you don't discount but don't get a guest.

Increasing

Earlier, we discussed that there can be seasons where your property can be priced higher, such as when there is a large number of tourists – during festivals, conferences, or even during usual peak travel seasons like Christmas. Aside from these instances, weekends are also an opportunity to price higher than your nightly rate, as demand for short-term stays are higher.

Seasonal Pricing

To do this, I suggest making a list of events, conferences, and other occasions that raise the number of tourists in your area. Before you set a higher seasonal price on these dates, do check out the rest of your competition and see if they do this as well. Also, consider whether your ideal guest is the market for those events.

I would advise you to implement Seasonal Pricing early on, as travelers tend to book early.

Tip: Here's a step-by-step guide to Seasonal Pricing.

Weekend Pricing

A good rule of thumb as to whether this will work for you is if the hotels nearby also do Weekend Pricing. As long as you're not priced way higher than most hotels, then it still won't deter guests from booking you.

Tip: Here's a step-by-step guide to Weekend Pricing.

Airbnb's pricing calculator suggests making a 15-30% increase when it comes to Seasonal or Weekend pricing, but I would again suggest doing 5-10% first if you're new.

Last Minute Pricing

The last pricing strategy you can implement is to adjust it based on your remaining available dates for the month. Remember, more supply—price lower, more demand—you can price higher.

The same principle applies when it comes to your calendar:

Farther from date – higher price

Nearer the date – lower price

What you want to do is lower your prices just enough so that your remaining unbooked dates would be filled.

Tip: Here's a step-by-step guide to Smart Pricing.

The four strategies above are the basics of pricing your property right, in order for you to make your income goal every month. As you get to know your market, it wouldn't harm to make your own pricing strategies, or hike up your increases, as you see fit.

Chapter 9
Getting Paid

Here comes what is perhaps the best part of being an Airbnb host – getting paid! Here's a simplified overview of how Airbnb payments work, and your options for withdrawing your payments:

A. How does Airbnb pay me?

Airbnb facilitates all payments using a process that provides both flexibility and financial security for hosts.

All bookings need to be paid via the Airbnb platform. Receiving payments in person (except for the Cleaning Fee) is a breach of their Terms of Service, which can result in both host and guest getting their protection void when it comes to cancellation policies, refund policies and other safeguards.

There are 5 steps to getting paid on Airbnb:

Host selects a Payout Method → Guest pays via Airbnb → Airbnb calculates Payout (less taxes and service fee) → Airbnb releases money to host after check-in → Host withdraws Payout

B. What is the best Payout Method?

You can choose the most convenient method for you to receive your payout. You can select from any of the 5 options below:

1. ACH / Direct Deposit – Airbnb will deposit directly to your Savings or Checking account. To sign up for this, you need to enter your routing number and account number. The average processing time is 3 business days.

2. International Wire Transfer – Airbnb transfer the money to your account through a money transfer system. Depending on your location, you may need to enter your account number or IBAN. Banks may charge a certain fee. The average processing time is 3-7 business days.

3. Payoneer Bank Transfer / Debit Card - Enter your name in as it appears on your official ID. Payoneer needs to approve your details before you can receive payouts. Banks may charge a certain fee. The average processing time is 1 business day.

4. Paypal – Create a Paypal account or have Airbnb transfer to your existing account. Make sure that your account is activated on PayPal before adding it as an Airbnb payout method. You will be asked for your PayPal account, which is an email address. Paypal charges 2.9% + $0.30 for every transaction, and withdrawal fees for non-US banks. The average processing time is 1 business day.

5. Western Union – You can also collect via Western Union. To register, you'll need to enter your full name (first, middle, last) in the Western Union system as it appears on your official ID. Fees will apply. The average processing time is 1 business day.

Many banking systems don't process transactions on weekends or holidays. If your payout from Airbnb is completed between Friday and Sunday, it might not be processed until the next week.

There can also be a Minimum Payout set, or a minimum amount of payments that have to be met before they can transfer your money to your account. This is optional, and if you do opt for this rule, Airbnb will hold onto your host payments until they accumulate to the indicated minimum. It's quite useful particularly if your bank charges for every transaction – you'll be saving on fees by withdrawing less frequently in large amounts.

Learn about Setting Payment Methods.

C. Computing your Payout

To compute how much you should be receiving, simply follow this formula, and add or deduct all that apply:

ADD	MINUS
Number of nights x Nightly Price + Extra Guest Fee	Airbnb Service Fees
Cleaning Fee	Currency Exchange
	Local Taxes
	Government Taxes

Conclusion

I hope that all the information in this resource will give you the headstart you need in setting up your Airbnb business. Airbnb is not just a lucrative business to be in, it's also a fun and diverse community to be part of. Meeting and hosting people from all over the world and making money in the process is an opportunity that has become available only recently – take advantage of it! Do consult this guidebook from time to time and you are on your way to becoming an Airbnb rentrepreneur. Good luck

If you did find this book interesting and helpful, it would be fantastic if you left a short review on the kindle page! Thanks again!

About The Author

David Leroux is a real estate investor focusing exclusively on identifying high returns Airbnb properties. Born and raised in France, he was trained as an engineer and decided to invest in real estate when he was 25.

While he kept his 9 to 5 job, he searched investment properties that can be rented on Airbnb as they had a much higher profitability than other investment properties.

Due to the lack of information to find the best properties for Airbnb, he developed his own method to systematically identify highly profitable properties (over 20% cash–on-cash return, $100K+ revenue per apartment) that can be legally rented all year-long legally on Airbnb.

He now owns 14 properties in 5 different parts of the world and quickly received the "Super Host" status on Airbnb.

After reaching financial freedom, he decided to coach hundreds of students who experienced a similar success. In 2017, he created Cash Flow Street (cashflowstreet.com) and made his teachings available globally on the leading learning platform Teachable by launching the first step-by-step easy to follow method to buy Airbnb investment properties. David's purpose is to teach people how to accelerate their path to financial freedom using Airbnb properties and retire in less than 3 years.

Are you interested in buying the top 1% of the most profitable Airbnb investment properties while complying to Airbnb cities regulations?

Register to my FREE online workshop at www.cashflowstreet.com

www.ingramcontent.com/pod-product-compliance
Lightning Source LLC
Chambersburg PA
CBHW031553210526
45464CB00003B/1286